المضنون به على غير أهله

The Mysteries of the Human Soul

English Translation of Al Ghazali's
Al-Madnun Bihi 'Ala Ghairi Ahlihi

IMAM GHAZALI

TRANSLATED BY
ABDUL QAYYUM 'SHAFAQ' HAZARVI

Qadeem Press

Qadeem Press

Qadeem Press Edition
Breathing Life into Forgotten Pages
www.qadeempress.com

Reprinted by Qadeem Press in 2026

Find our titles on your favourite online bookstore using the keyword 'Qadeem Press'

TO THE MEMORY OF MY FATHER

ABDUL JABBAR

WHO HAD A LOVING ADMIRATION FOR ISLAMIC MYSTICISM

LONG BEFORE I WAS BORN

Contents

Preface

The original Arabic work by al-Ghazālī is called *al-Madn un Bihī 'Ala Ghairi Ahlihi*, which is regarded as one of the treasures of Arabic literature. It won immediate popularity throughout the whole Muslim world, where it was accepted as an authoritative and one of the finest works on mystical expression. I have based my translation upon the original Arabic work by al-Ghazālī. Even while translating from one European language to another, it is sometimes a matter of extreme difficulty to find accurate equivalents. This is especially so in the case of the Arabic language, particularly in dealing with such an abstract and complex idea as that of the soul. The charm of the original book is more than can be translated into English, but here the main aim is rather to make clear the ideas and concepts that occupied the author's mind. If a translator thinks out afresh on the same lines and has control over his medium equal to that of the author, then why should not as good a result be obtained?

Having written the original work, *al-Ghazālī* can persuade his readers that he has cast a ray of light on the secret places of the heart and that he has increased by a mite to the sum of human understanding about the soul. His is no mean feat. It is a high art to distill the essence of experience into mysticism, and to do so is to contribute something rare and fine to a world sadly in need of it.I wish to thank all those who helped me while this book was being prepared.

Abdul Qayyum

Introduction

The question "What is the human soul?" is as old as man's first appearance on the earth. Almost every nation, each according to its understanding and knowledge, has tried to find an answer to this question, which is the basis of all the world's religions. Philosophers and scientists, ancient and modern, have endeavoured to solve this problem. Many have failed, despite long investigation and research, but the human mind cannot rest content until this question is solved, and so the search continues. The materialistic thinkers of the Western countries have denied the existence of any such entity as the soul. But, their explanations and arguments do not convince those seekers after truth to whose inner mind a voice persistently says: "There is something immortal." The contribution of the mystics in the search of a solution to the problem of eternity has been significant, but has never been properly recognised. Mysticism reveals Divine secrets which no other science can possibly demonstrate, so it deserves to be treated far more seriously than has previously been the case. *Al-Ghazālī* was one of the greatest mystics of all times, and it is his views on the immortality of the soul which are the subject of our present study. He is universally recognised as a leading exponent of Muslim thought, and his works reveal horizons never conceived before.

By making another mystical work of *al-Ghazālī* available in English, it is my sincere hope that non-Arabic-speaking scholars will gain an insight into the reality of the human soul.

Abdul Qayyum

Chapter 1:
The Meaning of Taswiyah (تسويه)

After taking God's name and praising Him, *al-Ghazālī* said: Some of the inquirers have asked us to cast a ray of light on the mysteries of the human soul. As we found their question based on sincere faith, and since we believed that they could be profited in a general way from the personal vision of the sufis, we acceded to their request and begged the Almighty Allah to enable us to be of real service to them, for all the human beings will eventually return to Him. He guides whom He pleaseth to His own light and rewards His believing servants for their acts of obedience in the spirit of generosity and encouragement. Asking us the meaning of the Qur'anic verse:

﴿فَإِذَا سَوَّيْتُهُۥ وَنَفَخْتُ فِيهِ مِن رُّوحِى فَقَعُوا۟ لَهُۥ سَٰجِدِينَ ﴿٢٩﴾﴾

"And when I have fashioned him and breathed into him of My spirit, then fall down before him prostrate" [TMQ Surah Al-Hijr: 29]

They first wanted us to explain what *taswiyah* meant.

How and When the Matter is Fit to Attract Soul?

We said: When the matter is fit enough to attract the soul, and consequently the latter enters the former, this entry is called *taswiyah*. That matter is the refined and specially prepared dust in respect of Adam and sperm in respect of his descendants, i.e. human beings, for purely dry objects like earth and stone cannot be kindled into flames, nor does a wet thing like water attract fire, which is composed of various component parts, but this does not mean that all compound things like mud are capable of attracting fire. It is essential that the earth be compounded several times in order to become suitable for catching fire. In like manner Allah, the Almighty, prepares the earth in a special manner till it becomes fit for vegetation, and when man eats it, it is introduced into the stomach, the liver receives the cream and essence of it and transmits it to the heart; the heart in like manner extracts the essence of this in the shape of pure blood, which is further purified in the form of sperm, as a result of the sexual intercourse, and when the womb receives it, it is assisted by the blood of menses. Then, the compound becomes moderate enough to be heated by the womb, till, because of its purity and moderation, it is fit enough to attract and sustain the soul, like the candle which kindles a flame and sustains it. When God finds that the best of moulds in which man is created is ready to welcome the soul, He, in His infinite mercy and love, is pleased to send the soul to nourish the germ. Man's life is the result of the fertilisation of a womb by a drop, which comes out of the marrow of a man's body. Then, this drop grows to be a lump, then a clot, then an infant, then a youth, and then an old man. Wonderful are the ways of God in creation, and the love with which He guides His creatures' destinies and gives them the means by which to strive for maturity by ordered steps and reach the end most fitted for their natures. God's grace flows freely. His blessings are infinitely more than what the merits of man can ever deserve.

The Meaning of Nafkh

Then, these inquirers asked us to explain the meaning of *Nafkh*. We told them that it means the light of the instinctive spirit, which, like oil, feeds and supplies the flame in a lamp. *Nafkh* has a definite form. The blower blows a breath into something. The wood capable of catching fire can easily attract the latter when air is blown into the burning wood. *Nafkh* is the cause of burning, but it would be wrong to think that the blower in this case is God, though the result, i.e., burning, can be safely attributed to Him. Sometimes by cause we do mean the effect of it, though apparently the effect is not a cause. God says:

﴿وَغَضِبَ ٱللَّهُ عَلَيْهِمْ﴾

"Allah is angry with them" [TMQ Surah Al-Fath: 6]

and also:

﴿فَٱنتَقَمْنَا مِنْهُمْ﴾

"We took retribution from them" [TMQ Surah Al-Hijr: 79]

Wrath implies a change in the angry person, whose aim is to inflict punishment on those who have caused anger. Hereby *Ghadab* (retribution) we mean the result of anger, and by retribution is meant the result of the retribution. Similarly, *Nafkh* here means the result of breathing soul into man. Asked further: what is the cause of the light of the soul or the light in the candle of the sperm? we replied: This is an attribute in the subject as well as in the object. By the attribute in the subject, we mean the generosity of God, who is the source of all our lives in this world. There is none like unto Him. Exalted beyond measure is He Who has given life to all creation. For instance, the sun casts its light upon the objects most fitted for receiving the light. Such objects are coloured ones. Air cannot receive light, as it has no colour. By the attribute in the object, we mean well-balanced and moderately-refined things. An object cannot be reflected from a mirror which is rusty, even though the object is placed before it. It is only when the mirror is not rusty that objects can be mirrored from it. In the same way when sperm is stable and moderate, God breathes soul into it, and there is no change in God Himself. It is wrong to believe that the human soul has no beginning. It is not eternal, and it is created when the matter is fit to receive it. Suppose a man looks into a mirror. His face seems to be reflected into it, though actually the face is not in the mirror. It is still attached to the body of the person in question. One cannot make use of the rusty mirror, not because the face of the user is incapable of reflection, but because the mirror itself is unclean and does not accept things to be reflected into it. Then, these inquisitors further asked us what Divine benevolence is. We explained that it cannot be compared to the container pouring clean water on our hands. The use of water consists in its elements, leaving the container, and washing our hands.

God's Benevolence

God's benevolence can be likened to the light of the sun falling on a wall. Some of the learned are sadly mistaken to believe that the rays of the sun, being detached from it, strike the wall and spread on it. The fact of the matter is that, due to the light of the sun, an image is formed on the wall, which is as bright as light itself. To illustrate this, suffice it to say that the face of a person is reflected into a mirror. Obviously, the facial features of the person do not separate themselves from the person concerned, nor do they attach themselves to the mirror. As a matter of fact, the reflection of the face, which resembles the latter in all respects, is created in the mirror. In reality, there is neither attachment, nor detachment.

The image so produced is a matterless form which does not exist by itself. It is impossible for the mirror of the soul to reflect in the imagination anything which does not stand before it. Thus, the whole sensible world, as it is thought and as it appears, is illusory. The soul is neither any particular state of matter, as it is considered by some, nor is it attached to it. It passes or rides over it and leaves matter as defective and powerless as it was. Matter, when it is fit for life, is blessed with the light of life by one Universal God, the Gracious, the Merciful. This is called God's generosity, which is no longer of the usually accepted order of His generosity, because God neither feels nor is He felt. He does not induce variations into His nature. No one knows the nature of His kindness to His creatures, since it is a Divine kindness which only God can know and do. Then, the inquirers further said to us: Having explained the meaning of *taswiyah* and *nafkh*, please tell us something about the mysteries of the human soul. What is it, whether it penetrates our bodies like water filling the contents of a pot, or is it like an accident (*'arad*) in an essence (*jauhar*), or is it a subsisting substance? If it is a substance, does it occupy space, or is it formless and boundaries do not contain it? If it occupies space, please tell us where it dwells. Is it reasonable to assume that it lives in the heart or ventricles of the brain or some other limb? If space does not contain it, how can an essence be without space?

The Reality of the Human Soul

Having arrived at the conclusion that no other problem arouses the inquirers' interest so much, or sets their minds to thinking, as this universal problem concerning the nature of the human soul and its destiny, we answered:

This question relates to the secrets of the human soul, and there seems little doubt that Absolute Truth is unattainable by the human mind. Moreover, the soul is a mystery unholy for men to know, and the Prophet (may peace be upon him) has emphatically forbidden common folk and laymen to ask and discuss such questions as are beyond the reach of their understanding. The thing in itself is subtle and beyond the comprehension of most minds. Imagination fails to imagine its truth. Consequently, its comprehension is restricted to the elite, who should not divulge it to those who are unable to grasp it, lest whenever their minds fail to comprehend it or to understand the concealed secrets of the spirit, it becomes a calamity to them. But if you are the seekers after truth with a major talent in creative thinking and an insight into realities, we would not hesitate to explain things in this regard. Know that the soul does not resemble other bodies either in limitation or in accepting division. It is not an accident, so as to necessitate attachment to the body like blackness in a black thing, or knowledge in the mind of the learned. It is an essence and can produce consciousness or intelligence, which is the important factor and only the property of the living soul. It recognizes itself and its Creator and knows spiritual realities. An accident does not contain these attributes. It exists independent of the body and does not accept division.

The Proof of the Non-Divisibility of the Soul

There is a reason why the divisibility of the soul should be rejected as contrary to rational necessity. Let us say: Is the soul of Zaid identical with that of 'Amr or other than it? If it is identical, it would be a self-evident absurdity, for each one of the two is conscious of himself, knowing that he is not the same as any other. If the souls were the same, they would be equal in respect of cognitions. But if you say that the soul of Zaid is other than that of 'Amr and that the duality is the result of the division necessitated by the relation of the two souls to bodies, we will say: The division of that which is one and which possesses no magnitude or quantity is evidently impossible. How can that which is one become two and then regain oneness? Such a thing is conceivable in the case of that which has magnitude or quantity. The presence of both knowledge and ignorance in the personality of an individual is an absolute impossibility, while they can exist separately in two different persons. An eye cannot be both green and black, while the eyes of two different persons can be green and black. This shows that the soul is an indivisible being. All the learned of all ages have agreed to lead the human mind to the belief that the human soul is a part of the universe, which is indivisible of course to call it a part is fallacious, since a part belongs to the whole, and here there is no whole. We can call it a part only in the sense in which we can suppose one to be a part of ten. When you have understood that soul is an indivisible thing, you should further know that either it occupies space or it is matterless. It is absurd to think that it occupies space, for that would imply its divisibility. It is a mistake to think of a thing which occupies space, and yet does not allow divisibility. This is against the rules of logic and geometrical science. If the individual atom is between two other atoms, does one of its two sides come into contact with the same thing as the other does, or are the two things different? It is impossible that the two should be identical, for then the two sides of the atom would coincide. For if A touches B and B touches C, then A will be in touch with C. If, on the other hand, things in contact with the two sides of the atom are different, that only proves multiplicity and division. If we could place the soul between two opposite things, it would be evident that it would touch either one or the other. From one end it would attain knowledge, and from the other ignorance. It means that it would know and would be ignorant at one and the same time which is ridiculously absurd. If we were to liken a spacious indivisible thing to the surface of a solid object, say, a circular table, we would be able to see only that part of the surface which stands before our eyes, while the inner, hidden part of the surface is invisible. There is no such thing as is visible and invisible at one and the same time. Only the part of the earth exposed to the sun receives light, while the other part remains in darkness. Any spot we can specify on the earth is brightened by the sun in day time and becomes dark by night. If a thing has two ends, it is no longer an indivisible thing.

The Attachment or Non-Attachment of Soul to Body

The inquisitors asked us: if the human soul is a spiritual substance, how is it related to body? Is it connected with or disconnected from it?

We said: It exists in itself, is not impressed upon body, and is neither connected with nor disconnected from it. These properties are found in a body, and the soul is not a body. A stone is neither a learned sage nor an ignorant infidel, for it is an inanimate being, and to judge wisdom or ignorance in a being it is essential that we should experiment only with living beings. The question of possessing knowledge or lacking it does not arise in respect of things which have no life. Then, we were asked: In which direction should one go to find soul? We answered: It is not limited by directions, nor fixed in a location. Accidents do not exist in it, because, being a spiritual substance, it is free from the imperfections found in the body. Again, they asked us: Why was the Prophet (peace be upon him) forbidden to divulge the secret of the human soul? We said: Because it is beyond human knowledge. People are of two kinds: (1) those who are laymen and common folk, and (2) those who are learned. Most of the common people have denied the existence of God, because of their ignorance; how could they be expected to believe in the existence of soul? That is why, some of the sects in Islam called *Karāmiyyah* and *Hanābilah* do not admit the reality of God and human soul, as it is laid down in religion. They believe that God has a body, for they hold that only those things exist which can be perceived. Since God does exist, it follows that He has a body. They are confused in their recognition, since the incorrect state appears to them like the correct one, while the height of complete proximity to God is concealed from them. Such a belief is not held by anyone of any insight, but by those who are ignorant and, having acquired some knowledge in their youth, did not advance any further. Some of them made some progress and arrived at the conclusion that God is not a body possessing form, but they could not eliminate directions with reference to Him, and we know that directions do not surround Him, as they relate to bodies, and He is not a body. Some of them rose still higher and believed that He is beyond space. Such people are called *Ash'ariyyah* and *Mu'tazilah*.

Asked why it is not advisable to divulge the secret of the human soul to those who have attained a degree of knowledge, we continued: Because they consider that the combination of the two, i.e., the attributes of God and human soul, is impossible. If you say that the combination is possible, they will publicly accuse you of the sin of polytheism (*shirk*) and say: Since you do not realise that there is a difference between soul's attributes and those of God in nobleness and perfection, you are an atheist, for you claim things for your soul which exclusively belong to God. Such heresy results from theoretical inquiries which are the outcome of stupidity and stumbling. Then, they asked us: Why do they consider that the combination of the Divine attributes with those belonging to others is impossible? We said: Because they believe that just as the owners of two different houses cannot reside in the same house, two things cannot exist in a spaceless space. Two black things are two only when they are in two different places or in the same place, but at different times, or blackness and motion in the same place and at the same time are two things, because of their different natures. If it were possible to speak of two black things in the same place and at the same time, it would be possible to say that each person is two persons. Then, they asked further: You have simply confounded us by adding more difficulties to the ones we already have. We told them that they should know that in this particular respect, men go to excess and exaggeration. Their fallacies arose from their failure to understand certain generalities. They thought things are different, in view of three aspects firstly, in their relation to space, like two bodies in two houses; secondly, in their relation to time, like two black things at two times; and, thirdly, in their relation to nature, like colour, taste, smell, coolness, and moisture, found in a body. Though they are related to space and time, yet they are different from one another in respect of their nature; therefore, taste is different from colour in nature, not in space or time, and knowledge is different from will and inclination possessed by the same individual. The difference here does not lie in space or time, but is based on nature. Thus, it would be clear that a place can contain accidents of various natures. Similarly, it is also possible that things of various natures may exist in the vast inner world of images.

Commenting upon our answer, they remarked: In all your explanations, you have tried to meet difficulties by raising other difficulties. You talk far above our heads and have left us in a whirl. It follows from what you say that the soul can be compared to God, for you have proved the attributes of God to be belonging to the soul. We said: You are sadly mistaken. How could the comparison be possible? We say man possesses life, knowledge, and power, and he can see, hear, and speak. These attributes also belong to God, but there is no comparison between God and man in these attributes, because they do not belong to God exclusively. His being free from the limitation of space, direction, and time is also not one of His essential attributes. Most of our emphasis would, therefore, be on the attribute of His *qayyānīyyat* (i.e., His unparalleled existence, which is not shared by any other being). This means that His existence is noble existence and that the existence of all other beings is derived from and subordinate to His existence, like the relation of light to the sun or that of heat to fire. They asked again: You have explained the meaning of *taswiyah* and *nafkh*, but you have not told us why God has attributed soul to Himself and called it " مِنْ رُوحِي (*minrūhi*), i.e., "My own soul". If soul is derived from Him, all universal beings proceed from Him, all universal beings proceed from Him. He has also said:

﴿إِنِّي خَالِقٌۢ بَشَرًا مِّن طِينٍ﴾

"Lo! I am about to create a mortal out of mire" [TMQ Surah Sad: 71]

Then, he says:

﴿فَإِذَا سَوَّيْتُهُۥ وَنَفَخْتُ فِيهِ مِن رُّوحِى فَقَعُوا۟ لَهُۥ سَٰجِدِينَ ٢٩﴾

"And when I have fashioned him and breathed into him of My spirit" [TMQ Surah Al-Hijr: 29]

If it means that the soul is a part of God, and man's body receives it as a gift from Him, like a beggar who receives alms from a generous person who says: "I have helped the poor man out of his financial difficulties," then it will follow that the personality of God, like the money of the generous person, is divisible, though you have already refuted this argument. We said: If it were possible for the sun to say "أفضت على الأرض من نوري", *[I have blessed the earth with my light]*, of course, it would be right on the part of the sun to say so. This would mean that the earth receives a part of the light from the sun, though the light itself is dimmer than its source. You know that soul does not stand in need of space or direction and that it knows all the beings in all their species by a knowledge which is not particular but universal. As God also does know Himself as the Principle of the emanation of all that emanates from Him, that is why God has attributed soul to Himself.

The World of Matter and the World of Creation

They inquired further: What is the meaning of

﴿قُلِ ٱلرُّوحُ مِنۡ أَمۡرِ رَبِّي﴾

and what is meant by the world of matter and the world of creation? We said: Said Allah, the Exalted to His Prophet (Peace be upon him): "They will ask you of the spirit, say: The spirit comes at the bidding of my Lord

﴿قُلِ ٱلرُّوحُ مِنۡ أَمۡرِ رَبِّي﴾

means that the spirit is by command of my Lord. All things which can be measured or surveyed are included in the world of matter and by the world of creation, we mean all things which depend on the decrees of God. His will is ancient. In its eternal nature, it governs the origination of phenomena in their appointed times in accordance with the eternal foreknowledge of God. Here, the world of creation does not mean the act of creating or inventing. Things which have no body or quantity are included in the decrees of God, resulting in the creation of the world of images and memories; the world of souls belonging to human beings, as well as angels, therefore, includes *'Alam-i-Amr* which means things which are removed from form and quantity and unlimited by directions and climes, in spite of their having existence. It is impossible to doubt the existence of this mental or psychical world, the extent of which cannot be conjured up by imagination. Then the inquisitors further asked: Perhaps you mean to say that the soul is not originated. It is eternal. We answered: Some of the sages and learned have slipped into this error. Their ignorance has led them astray. You can call soul eternal only in the sense that having no quantity, it is matterless form which is indivisible and which does not exist materially. You should know that the soul is originated and that it is not eternal. Refrain from speculations on the decrees of God. If we were to relate all the arguments advanced by saints and sages and the counter-arguments which have been handed down to us by philosophers and scientists, we should have to devote innumerable pages to the problem. But we prefer brevity lest the discussion should lengthen out and our attention should be diverted from the main question to its side issues.

Chapter II:
How The Soul Comes Into Existence

What must be taken for granted is that the soul comes into existence when the sperm enters the womb, that because of its physical constitution the sperm is prepared to receive the soul, which will be its director, and that it does not receive the soul merely because it is just a soul. In like manner a mirror which is free from rust reflects the image of a person standing close by. If the soul was one before the existence of bodies, how did it get divided? The division of that which has no magnitude or quantity is unintelligible. If, however, it is asserted that no division took place, still it will be an absurd assertion, for evidently the soul of Zaid is other than that of 'Amr. If the two were one, the cognition of Zaid would be the cognition of 'Amr, because knowledge is one of the essential attributes of the soul, and the essential attributes enter into all the relations of the essence. And if the souls form a plurality, what is the cause of plurality? This cause cannot be found in matters or places or times or attributes, for there is nothing in all these to necessitate a difference of quality among the souls. It is unintelligible, rather self-contradictory, to speak of an attribute of which the function is to distinguish something from its like. For by likeness is meant that there is no distinction, and by distinction is meant that there is no likeness. It is not proper to imagine that two black things in two different places are like each other in all respects. For "this" is in one place and "that" is in another place; hence the necessity for the distinction between the two. Norcan two black things in the same place but at different times be absolutely like each other. For "this" is separated from "that" in time. How, therefore, can the two be equal in all respects? When we say: "Two black things are like each other," we mean they are alike only in respect of the particular attribute of blackness. For instance, it can be said that blackness in an inkpot containing black ink is like the blackness of a crow. We do not mean that the inkpot and the crow are alike in an unqualified sense. For if that were the meaning and if the identity of time and place had left no dissimilarity, then the two black things would not be intelligible, and their duality would be absolutely irrational. The difference in soul before the existence of bodies is impossible, for the difference is of two kinds:

(1) Difference in kind and nature, like water and fire, whiteness and blackness, knowledge and ignorance.

(2) Difference in accidents which have no relation with nature, like the difference in cold and hot water.

It is absurd to imagine that souls are different from one another in respect of nature, because all human souls belong to the same category and are the same in view of their nature or reality. Their mutual difference in respect of accidents is also impossible, because when a nature is attached to bodies or is attributed to them in any manner, it becomes different as the result of contact with accidents, for there must be difference in the parts of a body, but when a nature is not attached to bodies, it is impossible to find difference in it. The problem requires a lengthy discussion for its solution, but we cannot afford it at the cost of brevity.

The Condition of Human Souls and Difference among them after the Death of Bodies

Then the inquirers further asked us: What becomes of the human soul after death? Do you think that there is plurality and difference among human souls after the death of bodies, when no sign of individuality is left after the dissolution of the physical form? We answered: This is not the same case as that of souls before the death of the body because in the opinion of the true believers the departed souls differ in quality, in so far as each acquires from its body a different proclivity. Before death its preoccupation with the direction of matter, i.e., body, results in knowledge and ignorance, cleanliness and dirt, good and bad habits. These physical qualities generate in the soul those attributes which are called virtues or vices. That is why the souls become different after death, and this is the reason why we believe in plurality among human souls after death. As all separate intelligences are within the Universal Intelligence, so all individual souls are embraced by the Universal Soul. They are all same, because all are an offshoot of the same Universal Soul, yet distinct in individuals. Departed souls require preparation of a different kind. It is not improbable that the preparation required by perfect souls, which have departed from bodies, should be different from the one required by souls which have come into existence for the first time. Before the creation of bodies, the question of plurality cannot arise, for there cannot be an imaginable cause for difference among them. Continuing, they asked us to explain the meaning of the tradition: "خلق الله آدم على صورته" and according to another version: "خلق الله آدم على صورة الرحمان" *[God made Adam like Himself, or God made Adam compassionate like Himself]*. We explained:

The Meaning of Şürat or Image

Surat (image or form) is a common noun. Some things are sometimes expressed through metaphor or allegory so that its impression on the heart of the listener may be deep. Its value is that it leaves a greater impression on the heart. This kind of metaphor belongs to the principle of expressing a certain meaning through a picture which contains the same meaning or a similar meaning. The knowledge that in such cases there are inner meanings which differ from the outward significations can be determined only either by rational or legal evidence. The feeble-minded will regard the literal exoteric meaning sensible and will not go beyond it, but the man who has an insight for realities will comprehend the secret it contains. On the authority of this tradition, a meaning other than the outward is intended. *Şürat* or image means here an intellectual and not a physical image. In it, those attributes of the human soul are mentioned which have been derived from the personality of God and His attributes and actions. Man and God are highly dynamic personalities distinct from each other and yet together. The human soul is a spiritual substance which is not a body possessing form, nor a substance restricted and limited. It is not space-filling and is neither connected to body nor disconnected from it, neither inside body, nor outside it. These attributes also belong to God. The essential attributes of the soul are that it is a pure intelligence possessing life, knowledge, and peace, and can hear, see, and speak. God also has the same attributes.

The soul causes human bodies to function in the following manner. Our giving a form to something in our soul is not sufficient for the production of the form of that thing. Accordingly, together with knowledge we need an act of will which appears as a new factor. This originates from the faculty of desire. As a result of it, there comes into operation the faculty which causes the movement of the muscles and the tendons in the outer limbs. So, with the movement of the muscles and the tendons the hand or some other limb begins to move. With the movement of the hand arises the movement of a pen or whatever external instrument there may be. With the movement of the pen arises the movement of the matter, e.g. the ink in this case. And then comes into being the form of the written thing to which we had given a form in our souls. And this is the reason why the mere existence of form in our souls is neither power nor will. On the contrary, our power is with the principle which moves the muscles. So, the form moves another mover, i.e. the principle of our power. Man's action is inconceivable without power and will. And will is inconceivable without knowledge. The power of writing is in the hand and the fingers, but the knowledge of it is not in the hand. Nor is the will in the hand. When the digestive and other internal organs of the human bodies have become fully developed, the heart attracts to itself the essence of the vegetative spirit, and having further matured it forms the life; the essence of this again is attracted to the brain, where, after being matured, it is developed into the soul and the remainder dispersed through nerves into limbs, where it becomes the source of sense and motion. In the wombs these developments occupy several months, before the body is actually born. The real self is connected with the body through the spirit, which is a subtle vapour-like substance spreading all over the body. And those who have carefully considered the actions of God, and looked into the wonderful ways of His creation, have arrived at the conclusion that He created the vegetable and animal kingdoms out of the movement of various parts of the heavens and stars, which are moved by angels. They are also of opinion that man is an agent in this lower and lesser world of sense, as He is omnipotent in the upper and greater world of intelligence. He has the power to create anything He wills. Production and destruction are the effects of His will. So, when He wills, He produces, and when He wills, He destroys. The most extraordinary cosmologies have been worked out, in which the various parts of the heavens, which are living beings composed of bodies and souls, are equated to different parts of the human body. In its functions the human heart can be likened to the throne of God, the brain to the soul of the highest sphere, the senses to angels, who have but to obey God by nature, the muscles and limbs to heavens, the power in fingers is as reliable and firm as a spirit inseparably connected with bodies. The compounded ink which man uses for purposes of solving sums in arithmetic, like addition, subtraction, multiplication, etc., is a mixture of diverse elements. Man's treasure house of imagination is the *Lawh-i-Hahfüz* or "The Preserved Tablet." The impression of the particulars of the world upon the souls of the heavens is like the impression of the memorables upon the faculty of memory, which is located inside the brain of man. Man comprehends his own attributes and, by comparison and analogy with these, he understands the attributes of God. Those who understand the attributes of God, as they are mirrored in the human soul, would understand the meaning lying hidden in the tradition:

من عرف نفسه فقد عرف ربه *[He who knows himself knows God].* It was also revealed to our Prophet that he who does not know the spirit does not know himself, and he who does not know himself does not know God. Explaining things further, we continued: What we find in the sacred texts is only an allegory proportioned to the limitations of common understanding, just as the verses and traditions with an anthropomorphic import are allegories used to facilitate understanding. If this devise were omitted, we would not be able to know God through the knowledge of ourselves and it would be impossible for us to reach our maximum development. The universe is the mirror of God and the heart of man is the mirror of the universe. The human soul is the masterpiece of creation, and the whole material world is placed under its control. If you then would know God, you must look into your own heart. If man had not been

Divinely authorised to act as God's agent in this world, the existence of the world would have been inconceivable, and man could never have learnt what God really is. Then they asked us: If the souls are originated, as bodies are, how would you explain the tradition:

خَلَقَ اللّٰهُ الْأَرْوَاحَ قَبْلَ الْأَجْسَادِ بِأَلْفَيْ عَامٍ، وَأَنَا أَوَّلُ الْأَنْبِيَاءِ خَلْقًا وَآخِرُهُمْ بَعْثًا، وَكُنْتُ نَبِيًّا وَآدَمُ بَيْنَ الْمَاءِ وَالطِّينِ.

[God created souls two thousand years before the creation of bodies, and I am the first of the prophets in birth and last of them in my prophethood. I was a prophet even when Adam was between water and mire.]

We said: The answer to your question is that this tradition does not prove the eternity of the soul. On the contrary, rational proof has actually compelled the intelligent to assent to the doctrine that the soul is originated. There is not a single branch of knowledge in which new terms have not been introduced for the sake of conveying meanings. Some of the sciences have external as well as internal meanings, so that some of the terms are obvious and readily understood, while others are hidden and become evident through research. We would, therefore, interpret this tradition in the following manner. By soul God meant the souls of the angels, and by bodies, the bodies of the throne of God, the highest sphere, the seven heavens, the stars, fire, air, water, and earth. You must know that man's body is a mere nothing when compared with the body of the earth, and that the body of the earth is smaller than the sun, which is again smaller than heaven above it. All the seven heavens placed over one another are greater than the ones placed under them, and these have no comparison in greatness with the highest sphere, containing all the heavens and the earth. The highest sphere is again smaller than God's Throne. If you can think intellectually, you will be forced to the conclusion that by bodies as mentioned in the tradition, the bodies of human beings are not meant. Similarly, by souls, the tradition means the souls of angels and not those of the human beings. If you had the knowledge of angels and souls, you would hold that they are like a great fire that kindles all human souls, feeds and supplies the spirit of humanity, as oil feeds and supplies the flame in a lamp. Each of the angels has an individual soul distinct from the one possessed by another. On the contrary, although the human soul is one by nature, it gets divided when it is related to bodies, and after its separation from bodies, it returns to its original character and is reunified. God refers to the souls of the angels in the following verses of the Qur'an:

﴿وَمَا مِنَّآ إِلَّا لَهُۥ مَقَامٌ مَّعْلُومٌ ﴿١٦٤﴾ وَإِنَّا لَنَحْنُ ٱلصَّآفُّونَ ﴿١٦٥﴾ وَإِنَّا لَنَحْنُ ٱلْمُسَبِّحُونَ ﴿١٦٦﴾﴾

"Here the revealing angel speaks in person: There is not one of us but hath his known position. Lo! we are they who set the ranks. Lo! we, even we, are they who hymn His praise" [TMQ Surah As-Saffat: 164-166]

and the Prophet (Peace be upon him) said: منا الراكع لا يسجد، ومنا الساجد لا يركع، وما منا أحد إلا له مقام معلوم" *[Those who bow in worship do not prostrate themselves and those who stand in worship do not bow, and there is none whose rank is not specially reserved].* Therefore, it follows from what we have said that, according to the tradition, the words "soul" and "bodies" refer to the souls and bodies of angels and heavenly spheres, and not to the souls and bodies of the human beings. The interpretation of the tradition أنا أول الأنبياء خلقاً وآخرهم بعثاً is as follows: Here, the word *khalq* means existence in a state of spiritual abstraction and not in the sense of creation in this world, since he had no formal existence before he was born. This was possible, because God's will is ancient. In its eternal nature, it governs the creation of all human beings in a state of spiritual abstraction in accordance with the eternal foreknowledge of God. This type of existence is the Divine existence (Existence in Him), which is timeless and which we have before our coming here. It is not the same type of existence as is usually attributed to God's creatures. It is a type of existence which only God knows, and only He is aware of. Now God, in recognising the Prophet's existence, saw him in the beginning, when he was non-existent and unaware of his future existence in this world. He caused, as it were, His desire to flow over him, according to His will, till he was completely imbued with Divine qualities and freed from the shackles of time. The life which Muhammad (Peace be upon him) lived in this world was without doubt the most perfect and penetrating. It was the most significant, dominant, and more adequately described as conquering, victorious, and truly overwhelming, as compared with the lives of other Prophets who had passed away before him. God gave him precedence over all other Prophets. That is why he is called the Seal of the Prophets and Lord of mankind. Nothing can be created or invented in this world of sense, unless the act of creation is preceded by an intention, i.e., an inner agitation. For instance, a mason intends to construct a house. For the first time, his vision embraces a perspective of his proposed great house, which is laid originally on the plan of his mind, at the back of which he has the number of walls and rooms, etc., and the order in which bricks are to be placed to make the walls. Unless he plans the house according to his prearranged outline, he cannot construct it. Similarly, know that God creates man, so that he may attain nearness to Him. This nearness is impossible without the assistance of the intermediaries nearer to Him, i.e., the Prophets. Prophethood, therefore, is not an end in itself, but a means to an end. God's claim to nearness is obligatory and binding upon all creatures because He made it obligatory upon them through the words of His Prophets, and not by reason alone. Prophethood becomes complete only when it has crossed a number of stages. Adam introduced it, and Muhammad (Peace be upon him) completed it as an Apostle of God. He was the one who had been made perfect by Prophethood and the one who had completed God's mission. It is absurd to believe that the door of Prophethood is still left open, for an addition to "completion" is a loss rather than a gain. For instance, a hand has normally five fingers. It would be defective if it had six fingers, for then it would not function properly and would be decidedly as harmful as a hand with four fingers. Though the sixth finger is something more than is required, yet in actual practice, it would contribute towards dislocation and confusion. The Prophet (Peace be upon him) hinted to the same truth when he said:

مثل النبوة مثل دار معمورة لم يبق فيها إلا موضع لبنة فكنت أنا تلك اللبنة

[Prophethood can be likened to a completely constructed house with a space left for a brick only and I am that brick]

When you have understood why it is obligatory to believe that Muhammad (Peace be upon him) was the last of God's Prophets, know that he was the first Prophet in view of his spiritual existence, and the last one in this world of matter. The tradition كنت نبيا وآدم بين الماء والطين also bears the same meaning, which we have already explained, for Muhammad (Peace be upon him) was a Prophet even before Adam was created. God created Adam with the sole purpose of choosing the best among his sons who could and did gain promotion to the loftiest height where the stations of the Prophets and saints lie. The revelation of Prophethood has different stages, depending upon the degree of self-mortification and upon the degree in which the inner self (*al-batin*) is clean and free of things other than God, as well as upon the obtaining of guidance by means of the light of faith (*yaqin*). Know that according to a Divine decree, first the fate of things is determined and then they are made, and the fate of all earthly things lies inscribed in the Preserved Tablet. A mason also plans his building in like manner and draws its proposed plan in a notebook. The treasure-house of things to which Divine power extends includes mysterious and wonderful things. The most learned are sealed off from their knowledge, and the comprehension of the greatest doctors cannot attain it.

Chapter III: The Pen and The Preserved Tablet (*Lawh Al-Mahfuz*)

It has been possible to conceive of the existence of the Seven Heavens and Paradise and Hell all written on a small "Preserved Tablet" or a small piece of paper and preserved in a minute part of the heart and seen with a part of the eyeball, not exceeding the size of a lentil seed, without the Heavens and Earth, Paradise and Heil actually existing in the eyeball or the heart or the tablet or the paper. It is not necessary that the pen and the tablet should be the same, as we know, for they are formless and only God can know what they really are. In spite of our selfless efforts, we miserably fail to imagine the nature of God's fingers with which He writes on the "Preserved Tablet". We also fail to understand how the tablet receives impressions like a hard and broad body upon which writing is inscribed, as children write upon a slate. For the multiplicity of this writing requires something extended on which to write. And if the writing is infinite, the material bearing it will be likewise infinite. Apparently, infinite body and infinite lines on a single body are inconceivable. It is also possible to conceive of the speech of God as being read with tongues preserved in the hearts and written in books without the actual existence of that speech in these things. For if the very speech of God should actually exist on the leaves of a book, God Himself, through the writing of His name on these leaves, would exist actually thereon. Similarly, the very fire of Hell, through the writing of His name on the leaves, would exist actually thereon and the leaves would be consumed. In like manner God is seated upon the throne in the sense which He willed by that state of equilibrium a state which is not inconsistent with the quality of grandeur to which the symptoms of origination and annihilation do not permeate. If these things cannot be explained in terms of the power of a powerful being, how then can they be explained at all? It is essential, therefore, that we should believe in them in accordance with religion. As a result of the deep search into the problem of essence and attributes, it has been found that God is the only reality; we are but phenomenal. Human attributes are only impressions and ephemeral mirroring faintly God's attributes which are eternal. Whatever the mind conceives is definite in so far as it is limited by place and time, but God is not a space-filling body and His life is timeless. The difference between God's knowledge and power and human knowledge and power is greater than the difference between any two things, for He is not composed of bodies within whose limits powers are diffused. His power and will and knowledge are one and the same as His essence. His life is not like ours, which needs for its completion the two different powers which are manifested through our knowledge and action. On the contrary, His life is identical with His essence. If His attributes are attributed to us, we would not understand them. Death is the separation of soul from the body, which is reunited at the command of God on the Day of Resurrection.

The Doomsday and the Resurrection of Bodies

The individual souls are part of the Universal Soul to which they will return. Thus, the individual's death is a minor return and that of the Universal Soul is the major return towards the Creator. The separation of spirit from matter is a mystery and the union of spirit with matter is a mystery also. As it is, we always misunderstand ourselves and rarely understand others. This is the end of our discourse on the mysteries of the human soul. The Prophet said: من مات فقد قامت قامة *[As soon as one dies, Doomsday begins for him]*. Here, the word *qiyamah* does not mean the Resurrection of bodies, which is a permanent entity to which existence will return after death. Here, the word *qiyamah* means the particular Doomsday, a subject which we have discussed in detail in the opening chapter entitled "Patience" included in our book called *Ihya 'Ulum al-Din* ("Revivification of Knowledge"). The general Resurrection of bodies will include all human beings and not a particular man. The time of Resurrection is known only to God, and He has not divulged this secret even to His Prophets and saints. It seems that the appointed time of the Day of Resurrection was not foretold for the welfare of men and for fear of the harm which might ensue. Though all times are equal by nature, there are certain times which are different from others in so far as the strange things created in them are concerned. According to *Mutakallimun* (Scholastic theologians), the creation of strange creatures depends upon the will of the Creator in any form He wills. Even philosophers do not deny the possibility of the resurrection of bodies, as they are unanimously of opinion that all created things originate from the revolution of the heavenly bodies, which are living beings composed of bodies and souls and that the higher and lower beings differ from one another in their attributes and functions. They also believe that bodies are governed by the heavens, the heavens by the souls, the souls by the various orders of the angels, and the angels by the "Light of Lights," who has dominion over the whole universe. It is not necessary that every preceding revolution of the heavenly bodies should resemble the one following it. They believe that it is possible that such a revolution might take place, as has no parallel in the history of the heavenly revolutions. This is the reason why such strange animals have been created in extra-ordinary times as have no resemblance whatsoever with others in the Animal Kingdom. It is also possible that the revolutions of the heavenly bodies may be suitable, but the beings which they create may be unexpectedly different. For instance, if we throw a stone in water, a circular wave is produced. If we throw another stone immediately after the first one, it is not necessary that the same form of the wave would follow, since we threw the first stone in the standing water, and the second in the moving water. Decidedly the second form would be different from the first. In this case, the cause is the same, but the effect is different, because some of the properties of the standing water mixed with those of the moving water. Therefore, it can be safely inferred that a time may come which is different from all other times which have passed. So, we can easily comprehend what Resurrection really means. Religion teaches us to believe in it which will be accompanied by the resurrection of life. You should, therefore, believe in the resurrection of the dead and the Day of Judgment, both of which have been mentioned in the traditions. They are real and belief in them is obligatory, because, according to reason, they are possible. They signify restoration to life after death, which, like the first act of creation, is within the power of God.

Attachment of Soul to Dead Bodies in Their Graves and on the Day of Resurrection

It is absurd to think that it is impossible for the soul to exist after the death of body. Those who deny resurrection or attachment of soul to dead bodies in their graves are the ones who are confounded and go astray from His path. In serious discussions no importance can be attached to such persons, and no notice ought to be taken of them. Death of the body does not cause the death of the soul, because the latter does not subsist in body. Rather the attachment of soul to body (during its lifetime) is astonishing indeed, for the soul is not in the body, just as accidents are not in a substance. The soul is not an accident, it is a self-subsisting substance which recognises its Creator and His attributes through itself and its attributes unaided by senses, for the things it knows are not felt. To call it an intelligence means that it is a non-material body. Every such being is an intelligence, i.e. it has self-knowledge and self-consciousness, and knows what is other than itself. It is so decreed that all the angels know all the intelligibles, without a single exception, because they also are pure intelligences not-in-matter. Man during his lifetime is capable of complete detachment from worldly desires. The soul abstains from carnal desires, turns away from the world and betakes itself to the struggle for the attainment of piety. If these conditions are satisfied, then, while it is yet in the world, its connection with worldly things is cut off, whereas the connection with things of the Hereafter grows stronger. In his initial stages, the mystic, by constantly remembering God and concentrating on the perfect, eternal, and absolute reality, loses even his self-consciousness. He gets empty of feelings - and even of ideas, He even ignores himself, as being now inside the Divine Presence and living together with it and having communication with it. His physical being continues, but his individuality has departed, though for his fellow-men he still has his physical body and appearance. This is a type of ecstatic state, of contemplation, inspiration and illumination, which is most glorious attainment and very near the goal of life a state of concentration, of unification, of liberation, of discovery, of heightened and intensified powers and withal a burst of joy, of rapture and of radiance. It is a point within ourselves, which, as the mystic holds, is equally God's central reality and ours, where spirit with spirit meets. One who gets rid of his senses, in order to meditate over Divine Reality, does not stand in need of his body or mind for spiritual subsistence, for it is the body which functions as the source of the diverting influences or preoccupations. When you begin to reflect over the intelligibles, the effect of all these diverting things on you will remain in abeyance. A dedicated sufi believes that there is no reality but God. His only recognisable desire is to pass his life in such a manner that his exiled soul is enabled to return and lose itself in its Creator, his only recognisable sorrow lies in the difficulties and distractions that delay the achievement of *fanā* (annihilation) - the passing away of soul's consciousness in the absolute goodness and beauty of God. Those who know the true nature of the human soul, which corresponds to the plane of the angels from where it derives real cognitions, do not believe in the soul's inability to separate itself from the body. On the contrary, they are of opinion that it is really surprising how a soul gets itself connected with a body. Know that attachment implies governance of the body and its functions. When man intends to write, he holds the pen and moves his fingers in the required direction. He knows that the intention is not in his fingers, but in his mind. Undoubtedly, if the mere appearance of the form of a line or a letter in our soul were sufficient for the production of that form, our knowledge too would be identical with power and, therefore, with will. But actually this is not so, because the faculty of writing is placed under the control of our bodies, and our power is with the principle which moves the muscles. So, it is not impossible for the Creator of matter and soul to cause resurrection of the dead, since restoration to life is nothing but a second act of creation, like the first one. Some of the philosophers who think that the infinity of the soul and the finitude of matter make resurrection impossible can only babble and show their perplexity, and are so bewildered that they cannot explain.

Belief in the Balance of the Day of Judgment

Again, belief in the Balance of the Day of Judgment, which is real, is also obligatory. Man should believe that God's judgment of the body and soul is just and in accordance with His will. On the Day of Resurrection, God will weigh on His judgment seat each act, each thought, each motive, great or small, with perfect justice. Our deeds will be weighed, and happy are those whose good weighs more in the scale than ill. If we do exist now, we cannot think of our annihilation or destruction; destruction in the sense of annihilation, especially in respect of soul, is impossible in this world or reality. We believe in the existence of the soul as a thing independent from the body, that it will continue to exist after death, and that when it sees its essence, it sees all and comprehends all things. At the time of death realities of all intelligibles are laid bare unto man. So, God says:

﴿فَكَشَفْنَا عَنكَ غِطَآءَكَ فَبَصَرُكَ ٱلْيَوْمَ حَدِيدٌ ﴿٢٢﴾﴾

"Now, we have removed from thee the covering, and piercing is thy sight this day" [TMQ Surah Qaf: 22]

The beginning, the ending, and the continuing are the conception of human minds that depend upon our conception of time, but we all know that time has no absolute existence. It is only a form of our knowledge, of our nature, as related to the experience of nature outside. This conception vanishes at the time of death. The manner in which our deeds will be weighed is that God causes to exist in the balance sheets of man's works a weight in proportion to the value of these works in His sight. Consequently, the value of the works of men becomes known to them, so that the justice of God in punishment, His grace in forgiveness, and generosity in reward might become evident. The balance is a kind of instrument with which greater or lesser things are weighed or measured. There are various kinds of balances in this vast world of phenomena- the popular scale for weighing valuable and heavy things the astrolabe for taking the altitude of heavenly bodies the ruler for measuring straight lines- science of prosody or laws of versification for composing poems- the knowledge of music or art of combining sounds to give them a pleasing effect, in which there is a system of notation, expressing the relative duration as well as the pitch of the notes. God has the power to make an intellectual or physical balance out of any material and of any form or shape. He wills in order to weigh our deeds. What is there to prevent one from consenting to the belief in the spiritual or physical balance in the Hereafter, when the existence of this thing can be safely inferred from the verses of the Qur'an. One should also believe that God will take into account all our good and evil deeds. This is why He maintains the proper record of our deeds, for it is inconceivable to think of an individual who lacks the power of doing beneficial or harmful deeds. He rewards His believing servants for their acts of obedience in the spirit of generosity and encouragement rather than according to their merit and desert, and He punishes those who do not stand one instant in contemplation of God and retain their interest in the causes of worldly pleasures.

Chapter IV: Intercession of The Prophet (Peace Be Upon Him)

We should also affirm of the intercession of the Prophet (Peace be upon him), and this was handed down in traditions from the Prophet and from his Companions. By intercession we mean the Divine Light with which the essence of the Prophet (Peace be upon him) is brightened, and this holy essence will cause light in respect of those essences which are related to the holy essence, because of their deep love for the Prophet (Peace be upon him) or their ability to translate the traditions into actions, or remembering God, with blessings for the Prophet. This intercession can be likened to the light of the sun. Suppose its rays strike the surface of water, and there is a wall standing close by. The light is reflected on a particular part of the wall, and not on the whole of it. This is so because there is a likeness between water and that particular part of the wall as regards shape. This likeness does not exist between the surface of water and other parts of the wall, which are left blank. If you draw a line from the particular reflected part of the wall to the surface of water lit by the sun's rays, you will find an angle formed (towards the direction of earth) which, if measured, will be equal to the angle formed in water, when a line is drawn towards the round and flat plate of the sun. It would be neither greater nor smaller than the other angle. This would happen only on a special part of the wall. Now, just as the special properties of a space demand a specific reflection of light, spiritual attributes also demand a light of Divine nature, a ray of

Divinity. Those who are governed by Divine Unity stand directly exposed to the Divine Light, which falls distinctly on their hearts. This Divine Light is a principle in the soul untouched by time and flesh, flowing from spirit, remaining in the spirit, itself altogether spiritual. In this principle, God, ever verdant, flowering in all the joy and glory of His actual self, appears. This light, this ground of the soul, has no earthly temporal origin. It is the same nature as God Himself. It is a point in common between the soul and God. There are others who devote themselves, all their lives, to the love of the Prophet (Peace be upon him) and follow what has been laid down in the traditions. It is they whose feet do not yet stand firm on the way to Unity. They are in need of the intercession of the Prophet, so as to get the required illumination indirectly, like the part of the wall which needs water for causing the reflection. In like manner, the intercession of the Prophet is needed. For instance, a vizier, being a reliable man, is a favourite of a *sultan* or king who forgives some of the sins of a person who happens to be a friend of the vizier. The person concerned escapes punishment, not because the personality of the vizier is identical with that of the king, but because the person, through ties of friendship, is related to the vizier, who is related to the king. Had there been no intercession between the king and the guilty person, the king would not have forgiven the criminal. There are several traditions showing that those who love the Prophet, i.e. pray for Divine blessings on him or visit him tomb or answer the call to prayer, or pray for him after the call to prayer, deserve the recommendations of the Prophet. This intercession means the reflection of light indirectly.

The Bridge Stretched Over Hell

We should believe also that the Bridge (*al-Ṣirāt*) is real. It is a bridge stretched over Hell, sharper than the edge of the sword and finer than a hair. The feet of the unbelievers slip on it, according to the decree of God, and they fall into the fire, but the feet of the believers stand firm upon it by the grace of God, and so they pass into an everlasting life. The utter negation of physical qualities not being possible, religion enjoins upon us the choice of the mean between all opposite extremes in morals. Tepid water, which is neither hot nor cold, aloes-wood, which is neither black nor white, the dividing line between a shadow and sunshine, which is neither shadow nor sunshine, are equally free from either of the two opposite qualities. One should neither hoard wealth, nor squander it away, for the one will engender avarice, while the other will make him a spendthrift. Similarly, one should neither shrink back from everything, nor meddle with everything, for the former is cowardice, while the latter is rashness. In the first case, he ought to aim at generosity, which is the mean between miserliness and extravagance; in the second, at courage, which is the mean between cowardice and rashness, and so on to all other moral qualities. The Bridge (*al-Ṣirat*) is the mean between all opposite extremes in morals. It is like a geometrical straight line, which has no breadth. The ones who have avoided opposite extremes during their lifetime in this world and have chosen the mean between them will safely pass into everlasting life, when they will be required to cross the bridge on the Day of Judgment. God says:

﴿وَإِن مِّنكُمۡ إِلَّا وَارِدُهَاۚ﴾

"There is not one of you, but shall approach it"

[TMQ Surah Maryam: 71]

God also says:

﴿وَلَن تَسۡتَطِيعُوٓاْ أَن تَعۡدِلُواْ بَيۡنَ ٱلنِّسَآءِ وَلَوۡ حَرَصۡتُمۡۖ فَلَا تَمِيلُواْ كُلَّ ٱلۡمَيۡلِ فَتَذَرُوهَا كَٱلۡمُعَلَّقَةِۚ﴾

"Ye will not be able to deal equally between (your) wives, however much ye wish (to do so). But turn no altogether away (from one), leaving her as in suspense" [TMQ Surah An-Nisaa: 129]

Since this bridge is possible, it is necessary to assent to this possibility in accordance with religion, and to stick to what the Qur'an means. He who disagrees with you and asks as to why one should believe in God, His angels, His sacred books and His apostles as well as in Resurrection will not be satisfied with a detailed discussion, while he who has been instructed in the orthodox faith disciplines himself in the etiquette of the Law and holds his peace in matters revealed to the Prophet without questioning the realities of these things. When you know that your existence has emanated from God and that you cannot exist even for a moment without help from God, the Sustainer of all beings, this knowledge will satisfy your mind and lead you to belief in God. An insight into Divine realities will also force you to the conclusion that you are such an essence as knows itself and its Creator, as well as all the realities of spiritual existence. If we hear millions of times that there is no soul, still we cannot be convinced entirely that we shall cease to exist after death, we cannot think of such a state. We cannot believe that our individuality will be lost after death. Such solutions do not appeal to our reason, do not satisfy the innate longing for immortal or deathless life with which cache one of us is born, nor do they bring to us consolation of any kind. Taking these facts into account, we cannot help but believe in the immortality of the human soul and in the Day of Judgment. There are two days for you, the one which you call today, when you are preoccupied with the requirements of your physical existence, and the other you call tomorrow or the Hereafter, when your celestial soul will have no connection with your body. When the connection of the soul with the body is weakened through constant worship, the agony caused by the soul's separation from the body will not be very great. On the contrary, it will learn to enjoy those Divine things which it will have discovered after the death of the body. This will shortly obliterate the effects of its departure from the world and its lingering inclination towards worldly things. The condition of the soul after death depends upon the degree of purity and knowledge it has attained in this life. A soul that is both pure and complete, or at least possesses one of these qualities, does not suffer long from being separated from the world, which is the object of love of most men in this life. It is only the soul that is both impure and incomplete or ignorant that suffers incessant pain in being separated from the world. God does not grant Divine knowledge to the common folk and laymen, as it is reserved for His chosen Prophets and saints. You should also know that this type of knowledge is mystical rather than reasoned knowledge, and this mystical knowledge is the highest thing to which man can attain. Some of the learned possess a knowledge which lies between them and their God, which they cannot reveal to anyone, as it contains those secrets which are beyond the confines of understanding and which defy description. This spiritual existence connotes their knowledge of God spiritually, without in any way postulating their being aware of their own individuality. When they attain to a state of absolute purity, they lose their personal attributes; by this loss, they are wholly present in God, they are wholly lost to themselves, and thus they are present before God, while absent in themselves: absent and present at the same time. They are where they are now, and they are not where they are. At the height of ecstatic contemplation, the soul is beyond itself, caught up, and the inner eye beholds the Divine Light without medium and attains an intuition of God. Now it is hoped that you would realise the value of ecstasy and understand how the Prophets attain to the knowledge of God through this medium, and how the Divine messages are revealed to them, when they are awake or asleep. This belief will further convince you that everything which has been mentioned in the Qur'an is true. When God wills to do a certain thing, He does it in two ways, either directly or indirectly through His agents, i.e., angels. It is not possible to give arguments about the existence of the angels, a secret the depth of which cannot be scanned by human understanding. But if you believe in the Prophets, it means that you also believe in the angels, for the former have affirmed that the latter really exist. You should be satisfied with this explanation regarding the existence of the angels, for, in the very act of trying to doubt it, you would be forced to admit its reality. God says:

﴿يَرۡفَعِ ٱللَّهُ ٱلَّذِينَ ءَامَنُواْ مِنكُمۡ وَٱلَّذِينَ أُوتُواْ ٱلۡعِلۡمَ دَرَجَٰتٖۚ﴾

“Allah will exalt those who believe among you, and those who have knowledge, to high ranks” [TMQ Surah Al-Mujadila: 11]

Physical and Spiritual Pleasures in Paradise

The things of the Hereafter promised to us, i.e., the physical pleasures like those of eating, drinking, wearing, and smelling, are not impossible for Divine Omnipotence; therefore, it is obligatory to believe in them. As a matter of fact, all the pleasures of this life dwindle into insignificance in comparison with intellectual and spiritual pleasures. But, people cannot be enabled to understand the latter, until they are symbolically represented through such things as may be observed in this life. This is the reason why physical pleasures like drinking milk, wearing silk-dress and eating bananas, etc., are promised to us. God created desires and placed pleasures under their control. There are many hypocrites who profess their love for God, but true love implies that the lover's secret shall remain untold in regard to what it manifests to the lovers of the visions of the unseen. The reality of love is the purification (*khalas*) of the nature of the spirit from all impurities and the annihilation (*fana'*) of self against all fortunes and interests. Those endowed with special spiritual qualities are those whose enjoyment of the vision of God on the Day of Judgment would be the result of their strenuous spiritual efforts. This would be so, since God would take complete possession of them, after removing from them both of their physical and of their spiritual perception. God says:

﴿فِي مَقْعَدِ صِدْقٍ عِندَ مَلِيكٍ مُّقْتَدِرٍ ۝٥٥﴾

"Firmly established in the favour of a Mighty King"

[TMQ Surah Al-Qamar: 55]

Anything which a man would like to have in Paradise would present itself in his thoughts of its own accord. The existence of the thing would depend upon his desire, and the moment the thing is supplied, he would be able to see and enjoy it. The Prophet said in one of his traditions:

إِنَّ فِي الْجَنَّةِ سُوقًا يُبَاعُ فِيهِ الصُّوَرُ

[There is a bazar in Paradise where people buy pictures].

Here, the word *suq* (bazar) means Divine generosity, according to which wonderful gifts would be offered to His believing servants. Suppose a man sees in his vision that there are beautiful streams containing milk, honey, and wine, which are flowing near a palace, the walls of which are made of gold and silver and decorated with jewels. In the premises of this palace, there are a number of trees, the branches of which are loaded with jewels, rubies, and pearls of rare variety. At the gate of this palace, a number of sentinels wearing dazzling uniforms are standing to welcome him. Now there are many types of those devoted to the interpretation of such visions, according to their own knowledge and taste. Some would infer the pleasure of gaining knowledge from some of the objects seen in the vision, while others would explain, on the basis of this vision, the value of ecstasy and the soul's struggle to attain this pleasure. Another type of persons would say that the vision foretells the victory over an enemy or his conquest of foreign lands or his visit to old friends, etc. Though all these states create pleasures, yet they are not identical with one another. Each of these is different from others in nature. Similarly, spiritual or intellectual pleasures promised to us may be of different varieties. There are two arguments to prove that intellectual pleasures are worthier than physical pleasures. Firstly, the state of the angels is nobler than that of animals, including man. Now the angels do not experience sensuous pleasures like those of mating and eating, etc. Their pleasure consists in the consciousness of perfection and beauty which characterise them, because of their insight into the realities of things and their approximation to the Lord of the universe (not in space, but in order of beings). Since all beings emanate from God in order and through intermediaries, it is obvious that the intermediaries nearer to Him should possess a higher rank.

Secondly, man himself often prefers intellectual pleasures to sensuous pleasures. For instance, one who seeks victory over an enemy renounces for its sake the comforts of home and hearth. Again, sometimes a brave man sallies forth to face vast hordes of warriors, because he holds the danger of death in contempt, being more absorbed in what he imagines to be the pleasure of posthumous praise and admiration for his intrepidity. One who is interested in the maintenance of his dignity and prestige hesitates to deal with his mistress in such a way as to be known to others. At last, he decides to preserve his dignity and restrains his passions, lest the contemptible passions should disgrace him. Obviously, the preservation of dignity is more pleasant to him. So, the intellectual pleasures in the Hereafter will be far superior to the sensuous pleasures of this world. But for this fact, the Prophet (may God bless him and grant him peace) would not have reported God to say: "I have reserved for My virtuous worshippers what no eye ever saw, no ear ever beard, and which never occurred to the heart of man." If you say that the things of Paradise which have been promised to us are intellectual or spiritual pleasures, which have no connection with body, and it is the body which feels the pains or punishment or the pleasure of reward, how could one reconcile these two contradictory doctrines?

Chapter V:
The Punishment of The Grave and Man's Suffering in Hell

Similarly, the punishment of the grave or our suffering in Hell cannot be understood unless we believe in the existence of our bodies after death. How is it that the corpse, which is dismembered, scattered, and finally reduced to dust, is restored to life in the grave or Hell? And if it is impossible to conceive of spiritual pain or pleasure independent from our bodies, how could you prove that a bald-headed serpent will devour the defaulter who does not pay the poor-tax or that ninety-nine snakes will bite an infidel in his grave, as laid down in the traditions, when it is an established fact that, after death, both imaginative power as well as spiritual perception are eliminated because of the death of the body? You should know that God's power is mighty and He is the doer of whatever He wills. There seems little doubt that absolute truth is unattainable by the human mind. That is why God sent His Apostles and showed their veracity through explicit miracles, and they conveyed His commands and prohibitions as well as His promises and threats, so it became obligatory upon all creatures to believe in what they brought. Refrain from speculations on the decrees of God. To add to what the teacher set forth is disloyal and unfair. The Prophet (Peace be upon him) is our teacher and our example, and we are his followers. This question disturbs the minds of those who deny Resurrection and believe that it is impossible for the soul to return to the old body, once it has severed its relations with the latter. They have no sound reasons to support their belief, and it seems they believe in the transmigration of soul, which is indivisible and which does not become incarnate or united with phenomena. A fact which is based upon the scriptural texts or upon the traditions should, therefore, be accepted. Some of the ancient philosophers have refuted the return of soul to body, but their arguments are not convincing and difficulties arise from their theories. On the contrary, the proofs of the soul's return to body have been definitely mentioned in our religious books, and we should believe in them. Some of the greatest philosophers have not denied the soul's return to body. In the general histories of Islamic philosophy, one usually turns to Abū 'Alī ibn Sīnā (Avicenna) as the most important figure. He has mentioned in his Peripatetic masterpiece *al-Shifa* ("The Book of the Remedy") that it is possible that some of the heavenly bodies might have been created as abodes to which the souls will return after the death of the bodies. He has reported one of his ancestors to have said that some of the learned who are not irresponsible and do not lack reliable integrity do believe in the return of soul to body. Had he not himself contributed to this view, he would not have regarded such learned persons as responsible and of reliable integrity, for there is nothing more unreliable than falsehood. Some of the research scholars have reported that Avicenna has merely mentioned this as a trick for escaping trouble or something unpleasant, for in his book of "Psychology," he has devoted a whole chapter to the discussion of transmigration of soul, wherein he has proved the impossibility of the return of departed souls to dead bodies. It has already been stated that when matter is fit enough to attract soul, the latter comes to the former. It is possible to effect resurrection by restoring the soul to a body, whether made of the same matter, as the original was, or made of the matter of any other body, or of a matter created for the first time. For it is the soul, and not the body, which makes us what we are. Two sperm drops begetting twins may be within the same womb and at the same time equally prepared to receive souls. These two souls emanate directly or through intermediaries - from the first Principle, to be related to the embryonic bodies. Thus, the soul of this body cannot be the director of that body, nor the soul of that body, the director of this body. This special relation can arise only from special affinity between a particular soul and a particular body. For instance, the body of one of the twins would not be more apt than that of the other to receive this particular soul, because they were two souls which came into existence simultaneously, and there were two sperm drops equally prepared to be directed by souls. The question arises: What is the cause of special affinity between a particular soul and a particular body? If it is a soul's being impressed upon body, then the elimination of the body will eliminate the soul as well. But if there is some other cause to explain the connection between this particular body and this particular soul (so that the connection is a condition for the soul's coming into existence), then how can it be improbable that this very connection should also be a condition for the soul's survival? Therefore, when this connection is severed, the soul will perish. And its existence will not reappear until God (Holy and Exalted be His Name) causes such reappearance by way of the reinfusion or resurgence of life, as religion teaches us in the doctrine of Resurrection. An exhaustive argument of this point would be extremely long, but what has been explained is sufficient and adequate. Suffice it to say that there is no proof for the denial of Resurrection, and when one cannot deny it, it follows that one has to believe inevitably in the punishment of the grave and Hell. If someone says: We cannot understand how the dead man's corpse suffers when it lies still and motionless, tell him that the punishment is possible, and neither the apparent stillness of the dead man's corpse, nor our failure to understand it will refute it, for a person in a coma or a sleeping person is outwardly still and motionless but he perceives inwardly pains and pleasures, the effects of which he feels once he is recovered or awake. Furthermore, the Prophet (Peace be upon him) used to hear the voice of Gabriel and to see him, while those who were around neither heard nor saw him.

Mutual Exchange between Virtue and Vice

It is also mentioned in the traditions that the virtues of the cruel person would be recorded in the deed sheet of the oppressed person and that the vices of the oppressed would be included in the record of the cruel. Sometimes a man who lacks the proper insight into the secrets of Prophethood fails to understand how and why this is done, and maintains that when virtues and vices do not exist any longer consequent upon the death of the virtuous or the evil-doer, how can it be possible for these opposite qualities to exist or to move from one record to another? If it is said that "deeds" being the substance are immortal, and they can exist independent of bodies, yet it is inconceivable how they can replace each other, we say that this happens even in this world, but we cannot see the effect here. It will be seen in the Hereafter as God says:

﴿لِّمَنِ ٱلۡمُلۡكُ ٱلۡيَوۡمَۖ لِلَّهِ ٱلۡوَٰحِدِ ٱلۡقَهَّارِ ١٦﴾

"Whose is the sovereignty this day? It is Allah's, the One, the Almighty" [TMQ Surah Al-Mu'min: 16]

The trouble with most people is that they do not believe in things unless they know them, although the things unknown to them exist in reality (regardless of their knowing or not knowing), and the true believer sees with his spiritual discernment that which the surface investigator cannot see with the eye of his head. It should never be forgotten that by the mutual exchange between virtue and vice is meant the effects of virtue and vice and not virtue and vice in themselves. The knowledge that in such cases there are inner meanings that differ from the outward signification can be determined only by rational or legal evidence. The rationale is when any interpretation, according to the outward meaning, is impossible. The cases where the inner meaning is determined by means of legal evidence are those which can be interpreted according to their literal and outward significance, but, on the authority of traditions, a meaning other than the outward was intended. The feeble-minded will regard the literal and exoteric meaning as sensible and will not go beyond it, but a wise man will comprehend the secret it contains. There is a Divine Light which shines into the very depths of man's heart, provided he separates himself from the followers of error and heresy and does good deeds. When he has attained to this supernatural light, he necessarily becomes free from all that is evil and is adorned instead with every good and noble quality. God and the world of spirits are usually interpreted as light and our process of cognition as illumination from above through the intermediary of the spirits of the spheres. Evil, the opposite of good, is unreal and dark and an obstacle between the supreme good and the individual soul. Good brightens the human heart, while evil darkens it. Renunciation and contemplation give forth the true light, until the mind, eye of the meditator, perceives the vision of the beauty of the presence, which at one glance fills his mind to the exclusion of all other sights. The sensible world is a shadow, and sin a thick veil between man and God. Worldly virtue and vice are stages in the development of the soul in attaining harmony. Since virtue and vice are of opposite natures, God says:

﴿إِنَّ ٱلْحَسَنَٰتِ يُذْهِبْنَ ٱلسَّيِّـَٔاتِ﴾

"Lo! good deeds annul ill deeds" [TMQ Surah Hud: 114]

The Prophet (Peace by upon him) said: اتبع السيئة الحسنة تمحها *[After every evil deed, do good deed, the latter will annul the former]*. He also said

إن الرجل ثياب على كل شيئ حتى الشركة تصيب رجله *[Man is rewarded for everything, even for the thorn which pricks his foot].* He further said: كفارات لأهلها *[Good deeds are ransom for bad deeds].* Every human soul can split itself into two parts at its own discretion one of which is Divine and high and is his true self; the other part is called lower or animal. Thus, the cruel man wants to achieve the objects of his carnal desires, which harden and darken his heart. As he was endowed with the light of good, which he did not make use of, he is deprived of the light. Since the oppressed person, being a victim of cruelty, suffers from serious difficulties, and is deprived of selfish desires, his heart becomes luminous, as the darkness of personal malice and greed, etc., is removed from his heart. This means that the light has travelled from the cruel man's heart to that of the oppressed, or that the blackness in the heart of the oppressed has moved to the heart of the cruel. This is how vice changes to virtue and vice versa. If you say that the change does not actually take place and that it is the effect of these qualities which makes itself felt, you should know that, as already explained, certain things are expressed through a simile, a metaphor, or an allegory, so that its impression on the heart of the listener may be deeper. Its value is that it leaves a greater impression on the heart. That is why sometimes it is said انتقل الظل من موضع إلى موضع *[The shadow has moved from one place to another]*, and it is also said: انتقل نور الشمس والسراج من الأرض إلى الحائط ومن الحائط إلى الأرض *[The light of the sun or the lamp has moved from the earth to the wall and vice versa]*. For instance, there is an excessive heat on the earth during the summer. A metaphysician would say: انهزمت البرودة إلى باطنها *[Cold has disappeared beyond the inner layers of the earth]*. This *inhizām* is nothing but a change. Similarly, people sometimes say: نقلت ولاية القضاء والخلافة من فلان إلى فلان *[The supreme justiceship or caliphate has moved from Mr so and so to Mr so and so]*. The true change is that which does not lose any of its properties, when it leaves its original possessor in favour of a new one, but there is another form of change which we call imitation change. This is permissible in the case of virtue and vice. To this subject, an attribute is attributed, and as long as the connection lasts, it is said that the contrary of this attribute is impossible for the subject. Therefore, he who subscribes to all this and believes in it without doubting will be of the people of truth and law.

Seeing God and the Prophet (Peace be upon him) in a Vision

People disagree among themselves as to the real nature of seeing God literally. God, although removed from quantity and unlimited by directions and climes, is nevertheless seen with eyes in our dreams, just as we see the Prophet (Peace be upon him) in the same manner. God's vision also is possible, just as it is possible to know Him without modality or form. One of the so-called learned men once reported that he saw the Holy Prophet (Peace be upon him) in a vision, coming out of his grave in Medina, and visiting one of the houses in the adjoining suburbs. None is more ignorant or misguided that such a learned man, for a thing or a person can be dreamt of in a thousand different ways at night. One can see the same man in a dream assuming various forms, i.e. young and old, tall and short, well and ill during short intervals, and the presence of all these qualities in a person at a time is impossible. Because of their stupidity no notice should be taken of such learned men. If it is said that the enjoyment of the vision of the Prophet (Peace be upon him) is confined to those who see the example of the Prophet, and not his real body, now this example would relate either to his body or his soul which is formless. If by the example his body composed of flesh and blood is meant, then the question arises: Why is the reference to his physical example necessary, when his body is already lying buried in a tomb in Medina? One who claims to have seen in a dream the example of the body of the Prophet (Peace be upon him) has certainly failed to see him, for a Prophet is a Prophet because of his spiritual attainment and not because of his physical existence. It is possible for a person to have a vision of the example of the soul of the Prophet (Peace be upon him), for that is his essence and his spirit and not his bodily existence. If you say if this is so, how would you interpret the tradition: من رآني في المنام فقد رآني *[He who has seen me in vision, has actually seen me]?* our answer to your question would be: The acceptance of the tradition which speaks of seeing the Prophet (Peace be upon him) literally is justified, because it does not lead to anything impossible, for sight (*ruyah*) is a kind of revelation and knowledge, although it is more complete and clearer than knowledge. This vision is a supernatural light, and its radiance has lighted the spiritual trail for hundreds of lives. The vision of his blessed and departed soul, to which form and colour cannot be attributed, is of an overwhelming nature and is an eternal gift which God has reserved for His pious and elect, who have been singled out for their extraordinary spiritual capacity.

Difference between the Meaning of Example and Resemblance

If someone says that he has seen God in a vision, this does not mean that he has seen the personality of God or the Universal Soul. This means that he has seen the example of God. If it is said that the example can be supposed in respect of the Prophet (Peace be upon him), but it is unimaginable in the case of God, we say that it is a misunderstanding arising out of the difference between the meaning of an example and resemblance. Resemblance is a thing which is equal in all its attributes, and it is not necessary for the example to have the same attributes in equal quantity, because human intellect is a thing which cannot be identical with any other thing in the world. It is reasonable for us to compare it with the sun, because both intellect and the sun have a common attribute -the light of the sun reveals to us the reality of the physical things, while the light of the intellect leads us to the realisation of intellectual realities. You can compare the sultan or the king with the sun, and the vizier with the moon. The Sultan or the king is not identical with the sun, in view of his body and attributes, nor is the vizier comparable with the moon in this regard. But the truth of the matter is that all the people have been placed under the control of the Sultan, as all objects that are in need of light are inescapably in need of the sun. That is why the sultan is compared with the sun. The moon is an intermediary body placed between the sun and the earth, so as to attract light, just as the vizier is an intermediary between the Sultan and his subjects, in so far as the light of the administration of justice is concerned. This is an example and not resemblance. God says:

﴿۞ٱللَّهُ نُورُ ٱلسَّمَٰوَٰتِ وَٱلْأَرْضِۚ مَثَلُ نُورِهِۦ كَمِشْكَوٰةٖ فِيهَا مِصْبَاحٌۖ ٱلْمِصْبَاحُ فِي
زُجَاجَةٍۖ ٱلزُّجَاجَةُ كَأَنَّهَا كَوْكَبٞ دُرِّيّٞ يُوقَدُ مِن شَجَرَةٖ مُّبَٰرَكَةٖ زَيْتُونَةٖ لَّا شَرْقِيَّةٖ
وَلَا غَرْبِيَّةٖ يَكَادُ زَيْتُهَا يُضِيٓءُ وَلَوْ لَمْ تَمْسَسْهُ نَارٞۚ نُّورٌ عَلَىٰ نُورٖ﴾

"Allah is the light of the heavens and the earth. The similitude of His light is as a niche wherein is a lamp. The lamp is in a glass. The glass is as it were a shining star. (This lamp is) kindled from a blessed tree, an olive neither of the east nor of the west, where oil would almost glow forth (or itself) though no fire touched it, light upon light" [TMQ Surah An-Nur: 35]

Now obviously there is no connection between the Divine light and the tree and oil. God also says:

﴿أَنزَلَ مِنَ ٱلسَّمَآءِ مَآءٗ فَسَالَتْ أَوْدِيَةُۢ بِقَدَرِهَا فَٱحْتَمَلَ ٱلسَّيْلُ زَبَدٗا رَّابِيٗاۖ وَمِمَّا
يُوقِدُونَ عَلَيْهِ فِي ٱلنَّارِ ٱبْتِغَآءَ حِلْيَةٍ أَوْ مَتَٰعٖ زَبَدٞ مِّثْلُهُۥۚ كَذَٰلِكَ يَضْرِبُ ٱللَّهُ ٱلْحَقَّ
وَٱلْبَٰطِلَۚ فَأَمَّا ٱلزَّبَدُ فَيَذْهَبُ جُفَآءٗۖ وَأَمَّا مَا يَنفَعُ ٱلنَّاسَ فَيَمْكُثُ فِي ٱلْأَرْضِۚ كَذَٰلِكَ
يَضْرِبُ ٱللَّهُ ٱلْأَمْثَالَ ١٧﴾

"He sends down water from the sky, so that valleys flow according to their measure and the flood bears (on its surface) swelling foam from that which they smelt in the fire in order to make ornaments and tools rise a foam like

unto it- thus Allah coins (the similitude of) the true and the false. Then, as for the foam, it passes away as scum upon the banks, while as for that which is of use to mankind, it remains in the earth. Thus Allah coins the similitudes" [TMQ Surah Ar-Ra'd: 17]

In this verse, the example of the Qur'an has been mentioned, although the Qur'an, being the most ancient sacred book, has no resemblance with anything. Then, how did water resemble it? Many visions were revealed to the Prophet (Peace be upon him) wherein he was shown milk and rope. He interpreted milk as Islam and the rope as the Holy Qur'an. There are innumerable examples which can be safely cited in this regard. Now, obviously, there is no likeness between milk and Islam, just as there is no connection between the rope and the Qur'an, but a man with an insight arrives at the conclusion that with the help of the rope we can get a far-flung object attached to the top of a tree or a hill. Similarly, by following the instructions contained in the Qur'an we can attain our salvation in the Hereafter. Milk is a perfect food, which is essential for our health. In like manner, Islam is a spiritual food for our spiritual well-being. All these are examples and not objects of resemblance, for there is no possible resemblance between these things. Nothing can resemble God, though He has a number of examples, which, owing to their spiritual capacity, lead us to His knowledge as well as that of His attributes. The First Principle, i.e., God, knows Himself as the Principle of the emanation of all that emanated from Him. He is the knower, the knowledge, and the object of knowledge. His self-knowledge being identical with His essence, He knows Himself as the original cause of all causes. In the state when the gulf is bridged, the Sufi realises that his own attributes are in reality the attributes of God, and so his own attributes vanish. He further realises that all attributes of men are only attributes in image-in secondary and derived sense, but that they are in reality the attributes of God. If man fails to understand the nature of his own attributes, he would also fail to realise the Divine Attributes. An example is permissible in respect of God, but resemblance is forbidden, as it is false. If you say that from our discussion it follows that God and the Prophet (Peace be upon him) cannot be seen in a vision in their real form, what we actually see in their example and not their true self; therefore the meaning of the tradition من رآني في المنام فقد رآني would be that "Who sees me in a vision sees my example," we will say that this type of existence, then, is without doubt the most perfect. This is because no human quality survives, nor does normal human existence continue in respect of the Prophets. As regards the vision of God, man is aware of his own failings and recognises his hidden fallibilities, but, nonetheless, continues to interpret indirectly and to rely on fallible knowledge, for God is unique, is single and exalted, and removes the true nature of His existence in the sight of man by denying him His vision. Meanwhile, He has allowed his worshippers to see His example in a vision. This is since God has taken complete possession of them. He has obliterated their personality and annihilated their individual qualities, thereby removing from them both their physical and their spiritual perceptions. If it is said that the example of the Prophet (Peace be upon him) can be seen in visions in accordance with some of the provisions laid down in the traditions, but there is nothing to show that the example of God could also be seen, we say that there is a tradition, according to which the Prophet (Peace be upon him) is reported to have said: رأيت ربي في أحسن صورة *[I have seen God in the most beautiful form].*

The Prophet also said: خلق الله آدم على صورته *[God made Adam like Himself].* This does not mean that God has an individuality, for He has no form or body. This means that it is possible for the light to throw upon the earth a shadow of an object that has a being. For instance, Gabriel appeared several times in the form of *Wahyah Kalbī*, and the Prophet (Peace be upon him) saw him on many occasions, although Gabriel appeared only twice in his original form before the Prophet. This does not mean that Gabriel changed to *Wahyah Kalbi*. The only reason that appeals is that the body of *Wahyah Kalbī* served as an example of Gabriel, for the revelation of the Divine message. Similarly, it is not impossible for man to have the vision of the example of God. God said:

﴿فَتَمَثَّلَ لَهَا بَشَرًا سَوِيًّا ١٧﴾

"Gabriel appeared before Mary in the form of a perfect man"

[TMQ Surah Maryam:17]

Actually, Gabriel did not change to man, in spite of his assuming the human form, before the Prophet and Mary. It is God Who guides man and Who gives the vision of what He wishes in the manner. He wishes, so that man achieves rightness and is in accord with Truth.

Many reports of the Prophet's descendants have been recorded to the effect that God, though formless, can assume any form at any time at His own discretion and there is none to prevent Him from doing so, but it must be made clear that God can never be seen in a physical form in a vision. The contact with Him is possible only through His example. This can never be achieved by any individual in whom anything earthly still survives, in whom the potentiality of an inclination to sin still exists. The vision of the example of God is the most precious of His gifts, it is reserved by God for His elect and pious. Their vision of His example is that which God inspires in them. Then, they attain true intimacy with Him and there grow up in them from God the qualities of existence and non-existence. Some of the learned disagree among themselves regarding the vision of God. Some hold the view that it is rude to say that one can have the vision of Him, while others maintain that it is permissible to speak of His vision. Those who believe that it is impossible for God to have an example end by saying things which are doubtful. But we do believe in the example of God, as well as that of His Attributes, and regard His personality free from all those things which could resemble Him.

And Praise be to the Lord of the world, and the prayer of God be upon Muhammad and his family and his Companions, all of them, and an abundance of peace upon them.

www.ingramcontent.com/pod-product-compliance
Ingram Content Group UK Ltd.
Pitfield, Milton Keynes, MK11 3LW, UK
UKHW021410190726
13845UKWH00028B/993